COUNSELS FROM GOD'S WISDOM

By Anthony Arnaldo Morant

If ever we should gain a true prospective on life, surely it would involve God's pathway of knowledge and wisdom that would draw all men to the infinity of God's own salvation, even though we might encounter various trials and temptations. This book captures the authenticity of God's truth and revelation, which testifies to His own character and, in turn, reveals to us the nature of God's forbearance and love toward mankind as He wishes for sinners to repent and surrender themselves to the power of Christ's saving grace and mercy.

World rights reserved. This book or any portion thereof may not be copied or reproduced in any form or manner whatever, except as provided by law, without the written permission of the publisher, except by a reviewer who may quote brief passages in a review.

The author assumes full responsibility for the accuracy of all facts and quotations as cited in this book. The opinions expressed in this book are the author's personal views and interpretations, and do not necessarily reflect those of the publisher.

This book is provided with the understanding that the publisher is not engaged in giving spiritual, legal, medical, or other professional advice. If authoritative advice is needed, the reader should seek the counsel of a competent professional.

Copyright © 2014 Anthony Arnaldo Morant
Copyright © 2014 ASPECT Books
ISBN-13: 978-1-4796-0450-0
Library of Congress Control Number: 2014911080

Published by

Contents

God's Own Character 5
Satan's Own Character 6
How to Build a Connection With God 8
God's Will for Man 10
Things We Must Stay Away From 12
Life Transformation 14
Complaining Distorts Faith 16
Hope in Regards to Christ 18
Never Underestimate the Power of God 19
Confine Ourselves to Perfect Discipline 21
God's Providence 23
A Life of Victory 25
Dealing With Sorrows 27
Compassion, a Metaphor for God's Own Glory 29
God's Response Toward Sinners 30
Finding Rest in the Arms of God 32
In Pursuit of God's Amazing Love 34
Walking With God 36
The Dangers of Separating Ourselves From God 38
The Weight of Sin 40
Why Keep God's Commandments 41
A Light to the World 43
A Mind That Is Fixed on Christ 45
Trust in Jesus 47
The Route of Salvation 48
Overcoming Temptations 50
Being Used by God 52
The Nature of Humility 54
Increase in Wisdom 56

God Honors Right Motives	57
The Chain of Prayer	59
Persecuted but Not Forsaken	61
Redeemed	63
Developing a Christlike Character	65
A Callous Heart	66
Meeting God's Expectation	68
The Power of God's Word	70
Self Ambition	72
Preparation for God's Kingdom	74
Protocol	75
A Message for God's People	77
Sin Ruins	79
If It Was Not for God's Grace	81
Who Receives the Glory	82
Does Jesus Care	84
Lessons Taken From the Holy Spirit	86
Emphasizing Faith	87
Love Surpasses Sin	89

God's Own Character

The work of God's creation is the work of God's own love and character in us, and without His works we would cease to exist.

The heart of God is love, but it is displayed through His will.

God gave us life out of nothing, and it is through Him we have our being.

God's counsel is one that exceeds the wisdom of man. It is the road map that leads to the road of salvation.

God's will promises us security in the context of us fulfilling His will.

God's purpose for us is to prosper, which is extravagantly demonstrated through the abundance of His riches in mercies.

God's love forebears and looks beyond the iniquities of man, grasping man's own potential to reconcile himself with God.

God enjoys people establishing themselves through His will that their lives might experience true success.

The character of God is a result of His love and righteousness.

God's timing is perfect, and He never fails.

The weight of God's power is measured through His love and compassion for each person.

God's grace is awakened by our own weakness, and His mercies delight themselves in our need for immediate aid.

God's good will is motivated by His promises and moral covenant, which are considered to be everlasting.

God's amazing ability to forgive far exceeds man's vivid imagination.

The mind of God expands beyond the realms of the entire universe.

God's trust is established through His unbending faithfulness, which surpasses all manner of doubts.

The love of God is transitional as it fosters to our care.

God's gifts are always furnished from the best. When He gives them, it is always according to His abundant grace that we receive them out of love.

Satan's Own Character

The power of Satan's influence deteriorates when our prayers are fervently lifted toward God.

One of Satan's biggest fears is to have God prove him wrong in front of the entire universe.

Satan's sin was a result of his pride, which gave way to his selfish ego.

Hatred is an avenue for Satan to enter into our hearts, but love makes him an outcast.

Covetousness is a product of the devil, and it will turn a man's heart into stone.

Satan's plans are not sufficient to give us life, but the Lord's plans will surely give us eternity.

Satan's choice of weaponry is doubts, deceit, and worries, which ensnare his victims in his non-progressive schemes.

Satan's life fantasy is to be like God, yet it will never come to reality because of its indubitable impossibility.

Give Satan a yard, and he will take a mile, for his ways are filled with presumption and cunningness to take advantage of any opportunity presented to him.

Satan is easily beset by the moral thought of God's established laws; to see one carry out the fulfillment of these holy laws fuels his hatred.

Satan's envy for Jesus is fraught with jealous rage and is so great his every intention is to destroy all who connect themselves to Christ.

Satan's greatest weakness is his own love for evil.

Satan's ways are always rooted in corruption, and his heart is immersed in the passion of deceit.

Beware of Satan's charm and cunningness, for his ways are filled with enticing traps that will lead our souls into eternal damnation.

Never trust a venomous serpent because his bite will prove to be deadly.

When God is able to give us relief, Satan will give us pain and misery.

Satan adorns himself with pride and high expectations, giving devotion to himself, which clearly gives way to vanity.

The character of Satan is weighed in lies and buried in his trickery.

How to Build a Connection With God

Loyalty to God requires a steadfast faith that relies on God completely.

If we would open our hearts toward God's love and kindness, there would be no need for God's wrath or judgment.

Anyone can attend church, but those who live by the Word of God are deemed real Christians.

What makes us a Christian is our own moral character in following Christ's teachings, which makes us disciples of Christ.

Man's moral character does not depend on his status in life but rather his confinement in God.

If faith reconciles us to God, how much more then will they who accept Christ as Lord and Savior be restored to His loving arms?

Living by faith involves a manifestation of God's words being transparent in our lives.

We can make changes in our lives, but if they do not include God, consider it to be self-driven.

Being true to God is to be disciplined in His words, whether others see us favorably or not.

Seek not the favor of man but rather to receive favor from God.

There is no way we can attain heaven without accepting the blood of Christ that was shed for us on Calvary's cross.

The power of faith is insurmountable compared to our most dreadful trials.

Faith demands trust in God to fulfill His purpose in our Christian journey.

Prayer will help us to keep in perfect connection with God; it gives us hope beyond the human imagination.

The more we share love and humility among ourselves, the more Jesus Christ's character is likely to be seen.

When we place our trust in God, the result of our devoted faith is increased confidence in God.

Faith makes the way for us to have triumph over the substance of trials in this world.

Only when our minds are confined to Christ's own character, then will our hearts experience what it means to be humble.

Love is more powerful than we can ever imagine or contrite, and it lives above all expectations.

God's Will for Man

A man's own way will not lead him to glory, but the will of God gives him the splendor he needs.

Humility will help us establish love among ourselves, and a kind heart awakens perfect charity.

As Christians, if we do not behold Christ, other people will not see Jesus through us.

The battle in the mind is the first victory to be won before anyone can ever obtain salvation.

The only way the world can be a better place is if each of us is surrendered completely to Christ.

The gospel is the Word of God put into action, and it is where God's eternal power lies.

Our own success depends upon God's unmerited favor that offers grace to aid each man's own progress.

Our stead in heaven will never be replaced if we would make God's will our own.

A true leader does not only lead, but he acquires new leaders in his stead.

Life can be complicated without the Redeemer's love, for under His counsel there is refuge from all despair.

A man's humility is a result of his own love and devotion toward God.

The Word of God is the seal of God's authority and approval.

Doing what is right does not include a wavering mind; having a clear mind to fulfill God's objective is what is acceptable to God.

Everyone has an aim or goal to accomplish in this life, but if it does not include God, then the purpose of it would have been in vain.

To love involves moral actions on each person's part.

The counsel that the Bible gives us leads to Christ.

This world was created out of God's love to establish a relationship between His creation and Himself.

The truth is deep, and no one can defeat it even if we try. Truth can go both ways—either we can accept it or discard it—yet it still remains the same, and there is nothing that we can do to it that can change it. The truth is the truth.

Things We Must Stay Away From

Malice helps the heart to become corrupt and gives aid to vengeance.

A dislike for God's moral righteousness will only take us to an end where there is no grant for eternal salvation.

We can never win someone's heart with hate because only love will prevail in the end.

If anger is the motive of our character, then it will seize to control us.

Sin can never have control over us unless we have consented to its power by refusing Christ as our personal Savior.

Never place your heart or emotions in the place of God's.

Doubts and worries have no power when faith is being manifested.

When we refuse to pray, the devil will have the upper hand over us.

A man's actions that lead to violence directs his journey to the path of evil.

If we decline God's will to follow Satan's wind of discouragement or snares, it simply means we have befriended the devil and made ourselves God's enemy.

If we think we are more intelligent or superior than God, think again; we are only fooling ourselves because He is the one who has established knowledge and has given us status in this life.

By receiving sin in our hearts, we have become its agent of power.

If we are guided by some other spirit rather than the Holy Spirit, it simply means that we are caught up in the snares of Satan's deception, which can cause us to lose our salvation.

What a man speaks from his mouth shows where his heart resides.

For us to show indifference toward the works of evil is to corrupt one's moral character.

The evil in a man's heart will only lead him to ruin.

Many have doubts that God is the Creator, but whether we believe it or not, His existence as Lord and Maker still remains a prudent reality.

Life is not about what position or possessions we have, but it's the character that God sees and rewards.

Life Transformation

True transformation begins from within the heart; then it is manifested on the outside, which clearly portrays Christ.

For transformation to exist, we must let go of our past sins and embrace the future with Christ's own righteousness.

We have no power to bring about transformation in our own lives because our own righteousness is like filthy rags; only by the power of the Holy Spirit can we be transformed into a new creation.

For us to remain pure and sanctified, our minds must be renewed through meditating upon the Word of God as well as applying it to our lives.

Being transformed involves living a life of sanctification with complete surrender to Christ.

When love becomes transparent in one's character, it is a work of moral transformation that gives birth to a new arising.

Before we can acquire transformation, we must receive justification by Jesus Christ through the forgiveness of sin, which enables us to be pure in the sight of God our Father.

Morality is in each man's nature as a gift which is bestowed on us by God that we might retain our virtue of character.

Changes that are deemed by God are supported by heavenly rewards.

Real transformation occurs when we accept that God has designed us to be moral beings and without immorality.

The greatest wealth a man can experience is conforming to Christ's own character.

If truth is cherished in the heart, then surely transformation will be seen in our appearance and character.

Holiness admits the changes that are brought on by love and humility.

If our words are coordinated by God's own virtue, it is a sign of ethical transformation.

When our hearts are renewed in Christ, then will the soul be transformed, awaiting the second coming of Christ.

If we adopt God's character and apply it to our lives, will it bring us salvation?

The state of transformation is a work of God's power buffered by His grace.

Complaining Distorts Faith

Complaining is a result of showing fear or exercising doubts.

When we complain it draws us away from the faith we profess in Christ Jesus and charters us an absence of hope.

We might encounter difficult trials and tribulations, but for our faith to soar to new heights, it involves boasting of God's goodness, which gives us victory through such periods.

Terror might strike in the midst of our lives, but love casts aside all fears and gives us rule over all anxiety.

Instead of complaining about our situation, we should have our situations complaining about us.

Complaining will take us a step backwards rather than carrying us forward.

When we murmur about God's protocol, our faith suffers and doubts hold our minds captive.

Whenever we complain or become unfruitful to what God wills for us, we become a snare rather than a blessing to God's heavenly kingdom.

Anger can set fuel to each complaint and drive our emotions up the wall, but a gentle response defuses the situation.

Complaining has a need for self, but trusting in the Lord gives way to charity.

When facing adversities and challenges, the opportunity is presented to make us stronger.

In heaven there is no room for complaining, but faith and humility is exerted.

Life's challenges can teach us wisdom, but our attitude toward the circumstances can bring about contentment or dissatisfaction.

Faith can never resort to complaining, for it establishes comfort in the midst of each storm.

Complaining about God's will won't bring us into His presence but rather draw us further away from it.

It is not so much about what you want to achieve but what God can achieve through you—so quit complaining and allow God to use you.

Those who have a strong will never find themselves without the need for God because their strength is impacted by God's power.

Hope in Regards to Christ

Jesus is the result of each man's salvation, for the hope He gives us revolves around the plan of redemption.

Jesus' shed blood gives us the right to enter the kingdom of heaven.

If we place Christ at the center of our hearts, surely our lives will be confined to eternity.

If Christ is rejected, surely our decision will not grant us entry to God's kingdom.

Jesus is essential to every person's well-being, including the restoration of each soul.

We are connected to Christ through the power of His saving grace, offered to us by His unmerited love.

The way to Christ is offered to us in love through the mysteries of His gospel.

The love that God offers us through Christ is beyond any measure.

Hope begins when our efforts are carried forward by our moral action to please Christ our Savior.

Satan has no control over us unless we give him the power by surrendering ourselves to sin. If we have given our hearts to Christ, we can experience the joy of freedom.

A heart that is rooted in Christ receives a badge of honor, which is worth its weight in purity and love.

The counsels of Christ's principles are the unmistakable truths that are fortified by His own character.

It is the will of Christ for us to have everlasting peace, which will bring a refreshing harmony to each man's soul.

Apart from Christ no man is able to receive salvation, for salvation begins with Christ.

A man's character is only valuable to him when it emulates the character of Christ.

A man's heart can never find peace in the midst of the storm; unless his heart is confined to Christ, he will be restless.

Christ is the bridge that connects us to God our Father, and His consolation is one that reconciles us with God.

Never Underestimate the Power of God

The power of God is established through the providence of His Word, for whatever God speaks it comes to pass.

God is not confined to the laws of nature or impossibilities as man is subject to limitations, for He is God and through Him all things are possible.

Never underestimate the power of God; as soon as we do, we are in for trouble.

God is our greatest comforter through every storm; He gives us refuge and strength to endure them all. He is our Ebenezer, a stone of help in times of trouble.

The power of God affords no compromise for those who favor or indulge themselves in sin.

The mind of man cannot comprehend the fullness of God's glory, for His power dwells in infinity.

For us to subscribe ourselves to the aid of God's power, self must be denied and God's will must prevail in us.

The power of God is a refuge for those who conceal and exercise their faith in it.

For those who are weary and heavy laden, the glory of God's power is able to give them rest.

Until the heart is surrendered to Christ, the power of God will not manifest itself through us.

With all the stresses of this world, only the power of God has the ability to sustain those who confine themselves in its rejuvenating power.

The power of God has the aptitude to either destroy or preserve life. Who is able to fathom the weight of His might?

The key to unlocking God's power is displayed in the arms of unmerited love and favor.

The wisdom and power of God does not relinquish itself to evil but confines itself to the purpose of accomplishing good.

The character of Christ gives us His perfect strength, which enables us to have victory through the midst of each trial.

The power of God does not submit to anyone's control nor is it a respecter of persons.

The power of Christ's resurrection is made perfect in His righteousness and love, which offers us the emblem of eternal life.

Confine Ourselves to Perfect Discipline

Being disciplined starts with fearing God and appreciating the ordinance of love, which is found in His commandments.

Abstain yourself from sexual immorality and allow the state of purity to define your impulse.

Make yourself available to the Spirit or else the carnal nature will overwhelm you.

In everything we must exercise temperance or else greed will lead us to ruin.

Disciplining the mind involves total surrender to Christ's will by giving Him full control of our thoughts.

The art of discipline is rooted in our ability to be obedient to God's commands despite the criticism or unwanted favor of others.

When we conform ourselves to the merits of God's principles, our lives will be redeemed as being sanctified through His grace.

Out of the disciplined comes strength and out of the insolent comes weakness.

A wise man takes heed to discipline, but the foolish ignore it and are subject to penalties.

For us to experience spiritual maturity, we must infuse discipline as a substantial part of our faith.

The ways of man are ordered when his criteria is fashioned after the providence of God's will.

Our fidelity to God includes moral discipline for us to remain faithful to His divine cause.

Our ability to offset sin relies on our discipline and loyalty toward God's profound truth.

Our struggles are not against the order of God's discipline or rule but against the structure of evil intent caused by sin.

God's truths must never be taken lightly but rather seriously cherished in our hearts.

Faith cannot reach its peak unless we exchange our faith for God's and allow His faith to reign in us.

The work of salvation does not exclude sound discipline, but it is reinforced by its power.

The affirmation of our faith lies in the balance of Christ's assurance and love, which determines our eternal destiny.

God's Providence

The moral state of God's words resonate through the eternal gospel, which is solemn to His truth.

God's care will give us sanction under His custody that will bring about refuge and hope.

The joy we experience from God is saturated by the splendor of His glory, which renders us with gladness and pleasures forevermore.

When we offer ourselves to God in love, His grace will respond out of mercy to acquire a relationship that will reconcile ourselves to Him.

The peace that passes all understanding is one that comes from God, which is our only hope to find rest.

The advocate of God's grace is portrayed through His Son, Jesus Christ, whose sacrifice has purchased us from sin.

The heart of God's moral providence resides in His own character, which displays the awesomeness of His unbending love.

The ultimate penalty of sin is death, but God's infinite mercy relinquishes in us the traits of sin along with its power.

God's emphasis is upon each soul to turn to the ingenuity of His love, which will fashion our character after His own.

God's humility and love surrounds Him with glory, which encamps around Him the presence of royal sovereignty.

Our mind is a wonderful thing if it gravitates toward the influence of the Holy Spirit.

If each soul is precious in the sight of God, then who are we to discriminate or relinquish ourselves from individuals? Is not God the author of love?

For God's love to be sustainable among ourselves it must be shared with everyone we come in contact with or else it will never experience growth.

A man whose heart is bent on hate can never see God because God is love.

God is the very definition of infallibility; He alone is perfect in all His ways, and His love knows no failure.

The state of transformation is a work of God's own miracle buffered by His own grace.

A Life of Victory

When we fear God, it is out of respect, and we must do so through honoring our commitments and showing the deepest love toward Him.

Do not let anyone determine your destiny, but let God be the outcome of your destination and reasoning.

The only sure victory we have over sin is through the power of the cross where Jesus Christ gave His life to secure ours.

We should surround ourselves with those who will help to motivate and uplift our lives, adding value to it; otherwise our character will be tarnished by those who seek to display negative behaviors.

Before we can seek to respect God, we must seek to respect ourselves first by not making provision for sin.

No matter how beaten or put down a man is, he can never be controlled unless his spirit is broken.

Being justified does not mean we are saved, for we are saved by consecrating ourselves to Christ.

Living a life of victory does not mean we won't encounter trials or circumstances, but rather, it means not allowing them to have control over us.

If love is not emphasized through our character, there can be no spiritual victory, for love is the power that unlocks all victories.

If there is no desire for God's character, then there can be no appeal for victory over sin.

We cannot receive victory over sin and still be partakers of this world and its sins.

If we were really lovers of God rather than lovers of this world, we would embrace God's truth.

Where we fix our minds is where our heart shall be; therefore, let our minds be fixed on Christ.

Let's not have a mind that is quick to judge or accuse but a mind that leaves all judgment to God.

Be careful not to refuse the standards God reveals through the providence of His Word. If you hold His standards in contempt, He will surely hold you accountable for it.

It is not good to disregard the truth because truth is the only source of freedom.

The Lord's matchless grace and mercies overwhelm each man with love.

Dealing With Sorrows

There are no regrets in doing what is right but leave all results to God.

Sometimes we will encounter sorrows, but it is best to take refuge in the Lord while in the midst of the storm.

Worrying about our sorrows won't change anyone's situation, but leaving it in the hands of God will bring about deliverance.

Satan can throw all sorts of problems at us that may harm us and yet fail because we have not succumbed to his power.

What makes a man great is the mimicking of God's own character, for his own character is insufficient for him to receive glory.

The joy of the Lord takes away our sorrows and gives us strength and comfort, allowing us to experience a part of God's glory.

If love is in our hearts, then hate will cease to have its moment.

If we knew the love of God, we would not exchange it for hate and allow sin to separate us from the love of God.

Unhappiness is brought on by a lack of desire or needs not being met, but we have the assurance that God will supply all our needs according to His riches and mercies through Christ Jesus.

For us to experience happiness, we must first stay focused on the positive things that help to empower our lives; give no heed to the negative or else it will give birth to sorrow.

There is no sorrow that is too big for God to handle.

If we would make God the center of our hearts, then all our sorrows would be diminished.

If we would surround ourselves with the eminence of God's perfect love, then our doubts and fears would commence to dissolve.

When prayers are offered with sincerity, the presence of God tends to give us comfort and strength through the midst of our trials.

When our lives are engulfed with misery and sorrow, we must remember the place where we first encountered Christ by setting our complete trust in Him.

It takes only the power of God to turn a sinner to repentance.

The love of Jesus is never too short to reach even those who feel that they have been forsaken by His love.

Compassion a Metaphor for God's Own Glory

God loves everyone and has compassion on the sinner, but He hates sin.

Our passion for God's will should be greater than our own so that we might live in self-denial, allowing God's work to be complete in us.

God's love and compassion for us is beyond the means of any power or reasoning.

Compassion is a result of us heeding the will of our conscience, which is guided by the Holy Spirit, moving us to do right.

Before we can ever obtain compassion, our hearts must be convicted of moral intent.

Our act of sympathy is endorsed through willful action driven by consent to God's goodness.

If we are not compassionate toward others, we are without a Savior, for Jesus is the center of all compassion.

Remember that God is always there for you when you are in need; He is never too busy to answer your prayers.

The acquisition of true riches does not lie in the art of receiving but giving willfully.

To love is to find God's compassion and humility.

God's mercy is a voluntary sacrifice that should not be taken for granted, as it is the power of redemption.

The means of prosperity should never bring about a change of character, but rather a humble desire to satisfy God's will.

Real compassion is not so much about sympathetic words but rather tending to the needs and care of others.

Our giving should not be based on emotional intent but rather doing what is morally right in the sight of God.

Forgiveness is the power arsenal of love; without it, grace would have no authority over the law.

The man who acknowledges he is sorry gives heed to correction and is considered wise in the eyes of God.

If love is in our hearts, then compassion can never be far away, for compassion is that which drives love home.

Only by faith, and not by sight, can we walk the pathway of salvation.

God's Response Toward Sinners

Devotion to God should never be the means to prevent others from worshipping, but rather the means to lead them to Christ.

God is never too busy to answer the prayers of those who call upon Him to be saved.

God's mercy is not confined to any form of segregation, but it is offered freely to those who choose to accept its potency.

The blood of Christ was shed for the remission of sin for sinners to experience the awe of God's infinite glory.

The love of God speaks every language, and at the foot of the cross, we are all at the same level.

There is no place that the warmth of God's love cannot reach us or where the hands of God cannot heal us.

In the eyes of God, everyone is considered a possible candidate for His kingdom.

Many times we empathize trivial matters and pursuits while the work of God suffers for our own selfish reasons, which, in turn, tends to separate us from God.

It was never God's intention that man should perish under the weight of sin but that his life should be redeemed through Christ Jesus.

Being saved does not mean that we won't sin; instead, it means that we have an advocate who is Christ Jesus to intervene on our behalf.

It is not a matter of age that determines our greatness but rather our commitment to God that portrays good character.

Our actions are a depiction of what takes place in the back of our minds whether it is of sinful or good intent.

For us to know God, we must love because God is love, and only by love can a multitude of sins be covered.

God will always love an individual, but there will always be enmity between Him and sin.

Forgiveness comes by acknowledging our wrongs and making amends for them.

For sinners to find peace with God, they must surrender themselves to Christ who is the giver of perfect salvation.

Finding Rest in the Arms of God

Though we might encounter trials and difficulties along life's journey, we are assured to find a safe place in the midst of Christ, where His peace gives us sustainability.

Although we bear the parcel of sin, the yoke of Christ will make our burdens light, and sin will crumble under its power.

We struggle not among ourselves but rather against the forces of evil that exist in this world. However, through Christ we are more than conquerors.

If there is love in our hearts, then we are guaranteed to discover eternal peace.

God will not allow more than we can bear; we can always depend on His capable arms to bring us relief.

It is not so much for us to fear those who can destroy the body, but He who can destroy both the body and soul.

When our enemies rise up against us, they will stumble and fall under the weight of the Lord's protection.

Whatever task God has called us to fulfill, He will equip and empower us to carry out His commission by all means because of His unmerited favor.

When our minds are weighed with temptations and doubts, we can rely on having the mind of Christ Jesus to overshadow the devil's schemes.

Walking with God is not an uncertain venture, for His promises are sure and His ways always prevail.

It is in God's hand that we place our trust. By His power we are kept safe from the assault of the enemy.

Only through Christ can we have the power to say no to sin and yes to God's own righteousness.

There is spiritual rest in the providence of God's truth to give us eternal peace if only we would confine ourselves to its power.

No man is saved as a result of his own works but by the finished work of Christ and His sufficient grace.

The avenues of peace all lead to one channel, which is in Christ Jesus who is the Prince of peace.

It is best to confine ourselves to God if we would choose life over death.

In Pursuit of God's Amazing Love

Before a seed can grow into a tree and give birth to good fruits the seed must be sown first before anyone can reap from it. Our words are the seed and the bearing of fruits is our actions working together in harmony, as faith and deeds coexist. We must acknowledge that we love God first, then after it must be displayed in our actions.

We were designed by God to love. It's a part of our nature as an inherited gift, but if it is not used, then our vessels are like a dried up brook that is in need of replenishing.

If we genuinely seek God's love, then our lives must be offered as a living sacrifice to appease the ingenuity of God's love.

We should always make decisions based on doing what is morally right in the sight of God and not allowing ourselves to be led by our own emotions or intents.

Seek ye first the kingdom of God and His love will draw nigh unto you.

Our aim in life should not be the paradox of worldly attire but rather obtaining God's awesome purpose.

While embracing God's love, we must take into consideration the love of others; by fulfilling this we are showing reverence to God.

It is necessary for us to apply the will of God to our lives to be deemed as prosperous unto salvation.

For God's love to excel in our hearts, we must make deposits on the accounts of others for our love to grow and increase.

The reward of receiving love is extraordinarily beneficial to both parties, whether on the giving or receiving end.

Victory does not depend on how long we have to persevere under trials but rather our confinement to God through faith, knowing that He will deliver us in His own time.

Uncertainty comes with choosing not to respond to God's high calling, which gives us eternal security.

If we are truly inspired by all the creative work around us, then we should want to be a part of the one who created it all: our sovereign Lord and Creator.

If it was not for God's grace, we could not give witness to Christ's intervention through the plan of redemption that we might experience the process of spiritual regeneration.

Walking With God

Our lifestyle should correspond with biblical principles to promote the purpose of health as it relates to our body, which is the temple of the Holy Spirit.

Our will power must be molded in firm discipline to have self-control at all times and refrain from sin.

Selfless generosity must be emphasized, for this is at the very heart of humility.

The Ten Commandments are like blinders that help to keep us on the pathway of salvation.

The best way to get God's attention is to display open love, for this is always at the door step of God's mind.

The best time to offer ourselves to the Lord is now, for tomorrow belongs to no man.

If we center our lives on our own initiatives it is impossible to walk with God, much less to know Him.

God's counsel is much higher than any man's intellect or reasoning.

When our minds are set on carnal things, it is difficult to find God because our focus is elsewhere.

How we might perceive things at times might not be as God intended, but by acknowledging God in all our ways and leaning not on our own understanding, He will direct our path.

For anyone to establish a relationship, it requires constant communication between both parties. That is why a daily devotion with God is necessary.

It is easier to follow God's commandments than to reconcile ourselves with sin.

When we are walking with God, we should be more concerned about spiritual matters than the allure of this world and what it has to offer us.

If we are willing to take off self and put on Christ's righteousness, the Lord will be satisfied.

If we truly love God, we should share the gospel with others, for this is God's method of communicating His love to a dying world.

By obeying God out of love, we can be faithful disciples to Christ and His sovereignty.

Hatred for evil is recommended among the wise, but evil is a stumbling block for the foolish.

The Dangers of Separating Ourselves From God

If we choose to sin continuously against God, He will seek to remove His protection from us.

Living in a cruel world without Christ can be like being between a rock and a hard place, where ones hope diminishes.

If we allow our minds to be controlled by the influence of Satan then it will be difficult for us to accept what is morally right before God as we are blinded by Satan's deceits, which only lead us to ruin.

If there is no connection between us and God then we can't be heirs to God's eternal kingdom.

A sheep without a shepherd is surely prey among wolves.

Without the intake of Christ's knowledge, we can never experience spiritual growth for ourselves; it is only the Word of God that has the power to transform lives.

There is much harm in being unequally yoked for this can tarnish the Christian's character because of separate interests among both parties.

Finding time to commune with God is as vital as inhaling fresh air.

The harboring of hatred in our hearts is related to a multitude of sins, but forgiveness covers our shortcomings.

The love of money will sever us from God, but if we put God above financial means, then our priorities are right.

The pride of life is steered toward vanity, and the lust of the flesh manifests itself in sexual immorality, while the lust of the eyes covets and distorts.

If there is no trust in God, then our faith is relinquished by doubt.

Hesitating to do God's will can separate us from His plan, for He is the one that sustains our life.

Abusing God's grace can move us away from Him, leaving us to our own depraved minds.

Anything that we put before God is an idol and should be cast aside, giving way to God's dominion.

Sympathizing with Satan will only bring us ruin, but aligning ourselves with God will impart unto us perfect salvation.

Time spent on things that have no worth to God should be invested toward glorifying God.

The Weight of Sin

The current of sin pulls us toward the stream of eternal death where no soul can ever exist.

Sin corrupts the heart and takes captive the mind; if left unchallenged it will ruin the soul.

When temptation arises our minds should be so in tune with God's wholesome character that sin loses its power upon approach.

The strength in sin is if we desire to endeavor in its venality.

Long-term exposure to sin can lead to spiritual blindness, where distinguishing between right and wrong becomes difficult.

The yoke of sin can only be broken through the power of Christ's intervention, which gives us amnesty from sin.

Overcoming sin lies in the balance of Christ's power to give us victory over sin through faith.

The key to defeating the adversary's attempts to control us is to submit to faith in Christ's unyielding love.

If there is unwavering love in our hearts, then sin is unable to find its way in unless we surrender to its power.

There is much virtue in restraining ourselves from sin because only the wise will inherit the kingdom of God.

Conform not yourself to the ways of sin, but renew your mind by imitating the essence of God's love and character.

The weight of our sins was carried to the cross, and there its power was defeated through Christ offering Himself as a living sacrifice, providing remission for our sins.

It is a burden to carry sin in our hearts, but with joy, the hope of relief comes through forgiveness.

Anxiety is fashioned by sin, but if we would learn to practice love with all sincerity, then the by-product of fear would be thrown aside.

When faced with harsh circumstances, it's best to petition the throne of God, bringing our needs and cares before Him.

Why Keep God's Commandments

The law is the fulfillment of God's love displayed through His very own character; those who obey the law shall make heaven their dwelling place.

Life is complicated without obedience to God's law, for the law is like unto us a navigational system that carefully instructs us where we are to go as it relates to the journey of eternal salvation.

It is not for us to follow the letter of the law but rather the Spirit of the law, which is love, for love is the fulfillment of the law.

If we resent God's law, then we cut off our prayer connection with God.

Upholding the law will bring a man in closer connection with God until his ways and virtues are fused with God's.

It is the law that helps us to be aware of sin as a mirror would reflect our image.

The law was sanctioned under God's own character that through obeying them we might display the sustenance of His moral character.

When the law is kept, the mind is renewed by its power, which is generated through love that helps us to exert a clear conscience.

If there is no law, surely there will be no order or peace, only chaos.

God's laws are not burdensome or difficult to keep, but rather a delight that keeps the channel of love flowing between us.

A person's loyalty and faithfulness can be found in upholding the standards of the law, which proves them to be worthy.

When it comes to keeping the law, there can be no negotiation or compromise.

Life is not about having our own way but learning to be satisfied through obeying God's law, which defines our capacity in humility.

Since sin is the transgression of the law, only by keeping the law can we escape sin through the power of Christ.

Although the heart of the law is love, it still demands justice as the penalty of sin brings death, but God's grace is able to supersede the law.

A Light to the World

Because of our faith in Christ Jesus what we have to offer the world is much greater than any man's expectation or hope.

By renouncing our sins and shame, we have become sentinels for God's truth with a mission to share the gospel with a dying world.

The light that we have received from God is His moral truth, which resides in our faith as a precious gift from God to illuminate our pathway unto salvation.

No amount of wealth can earn our way to God's kingdom, but if we purposely exchange our sins for God's renewal and take upon ourselves His marvelous light, then the gateway to heaven's door will be freely open to us.

The knowledge and wisdom we receive of God should be applied to our daily lives as a living testimony to God's glory and favor.

If we are partakers of this world, the world can receive no useful help from us as we become a part of the problem this world faces today. But if we reflect His character, His love will impact this world.

If we are pilgrims of the light, then the banner of its truth should be seen in our actions and spoken from our lips as it relates to Christ's love and character.

We are a beacon to God's light as we exploit His truth; surely we will become changed as we behold His fountain of truth.

What purpose does our light serve if it is not being shared with others? If we keep it to ourselves, surely its flame will go out.

We are God's instrument for reaching out to those who are lost and without hope in this world, so therefore we are messengers of His grace imparted to this world's care.

If there is only darkness in this world, then evil would persevere, but if there is only light, then good will prevail.

With each kindness that is exerted between us, God receives the glory; when humility is expressed in God's love, it is seen.

Only the light can succeed against the darkness, and only love can overcome hate; we must yield ourselves to the greater power, which is in Christ Jesus, that we might have total victory over sin.

There is no greater light than the love that Christ portrays, which is worth its weight in eternity.

A Mind That Is Fixed on Christ

The carnal mind sets its hope on worldly aspirations while a mind that is in Christ is driven toward heaven.

If our minds are drawn toward sinful content, it simply means that our minds are held captive by sins constraints.

The quest of developing Christ's character begins with our minds being fixed upon His forbearing personality and love, and then making them applicable to our own lives.

If there is a pull toward attaining perfection, then our minds are corresponding with the motives Christ intended for us to enhance our salvation.

When the world seems like it is crashing around us, our eyes should behold our beloved Savior—through the midst of the storm, we will find peace.

Sometimes when things do not work out as we intended it seems to meet the divine consolation that God willfully seeks something better for us.

When our sight is spiritually oriented on Christ's profound will, only then will our hearts be in tune with His.

When our minds are fixed on Christ, nothing else should matter for what is before us pertaining to God's will is much greater than any man's will or opinion.

An encounter with Jesus means an opportunity of a lifetime where the choice of choosing eternity is offered to us out of grace to snatch us from the burning fire.

If we would learn to love each other as Christ does, there would be no need for segregation or hate; instead peace would triumph over evil.

If there is a passion for Christ's love, then there must be a thirst for humility and a hunger for God's goodwill.

Feasting on God's Word will only draw us closer to the knowledge of God's love and character, which will teach us of His plan to redeem us from sin through the intercessory power of Jesus Christ our Savior.

There is nothing to gain if our hearts are in the wrong place, where Christ is blotted out and sin is welcome.

It is best to obey God's instructions rather than to give in to man's influence or reasoning.

The way to Jesus' heart is to accept the love He gives us; we are then to return it with love, for this is a portion of God's love.

Trust in Jesus

Putting our trust in God involves exercising hope, even if we are unable to see the results ahead.

When all other hope has failed us, remember that Jesus will never leave or forsake us; His ways are beyond the failures of man, and His promises are always dependable.

Worrying is not a part of God's nature. It is a method Satan uses to drive fear or doubts so that we might not manifest faith, thereby missing the mark of God.

Can a man worry to save his own life or give aid to doubts to suit his own sorrows? These are harmful to the human soul.

Giving ourselves over to anger can lead us toward resenting God and His providence.

Difficulties will arise, but trusting in God prepares the way for us to receive total victory.

Though we are perplexed and troubled on all sides with the constraints of life, Jesus gives us the assurance of His love and mercies that we might take refuge in Him.

If we delight ourselves in the Lord, then nothing would be too hard for us to endure under His banner of strength.

Our trust in Jesus proves how much He means to us and shows us how much it takes to love Him in return.

Often times we rely on others to give us support, yet they lack the virtue in giving. Jesus is able to supply all our needs according to His grace and riches in mercies.

Those who put their hope in Christ will experience trials and tribulations of all kinds because they have become a driving force against every manner of evil.

Confining ourselves to Christ's own purpose will endorse our spiritual growth, connecting us to newer heights.

It is always right to heed the counsel of God rather than to give way to Satan's snare, for this is where the victory is won.

When there is a genuine sacrifice made to accomplish God's will, it serves the purpose of loyalty and trust where God is concerned.

If we choose to resent God's truth, then we have made ourselves to be unworthy of His trust.

Our spiritual vigor lies in trusting Jesus as He intertwines His virtue, giving stability and support.

The Route to Salvation

An honest man builds his statue by being resolute to the truth, which makes his character a candidate for solemn truth.

Where salvation is concerned, all roads lead to Christ, for He is the fountain of youth that springs forth eternal life.

The foolish man loves to be misled, but the wise man is satisfied with the counsel that comes from God.

We have been given the power to live a just life that is constant with the teachings and principles of Christ our Savior.

God's promises are final, and yet they come with conditions in the realms of exercising faith, which unlocks them for us to achieve favor from God.

It is better to suffer under Satan than to be troubled by the hand of God.

A person who is acquainted with God is not an ordinary person by the world's standards but is one who represents God's glory and honor in heavenly realms.

It takes absolute determination and faith to remain loyal to God as we endeavor to keep His commandments.

The fragrance of God's love is hospitality; when we share acts of kindness toward other individuals, it reveals the meekness of God's love.

It is God's love that opens the way for salvation to come into our hearts, that we might experience His glory in humility and compassion.

There is no short route to the kingdom of heaven—it takes a total surrender of self and a life-time commitment before we can even consider ourselves a royal citizen of the heavenly kingdom.

If we would conduct ourselves in righteousness and not give way to sin's own demise, then we will gain the hope of inheriting God's kingdom.

Doing God's will is essential toward gaining salvation because His will is the representative of His character.

Salvation is offered to us freely through the personal sacrifice Jesus made for us on the cross of Calvary where the devil received a deadly wound to his claim on mankind.

A man's moral character has so much to do with his trust for Christ that it sustains him.

Overcoming Temptations

A thousand snares can be hurled at us, but they have no power unless sin is cherished in our hearts.

Satan and his evil angels attempt to lead many astray through sin as they fill our minds with deceitful temptations, which, when carried in the heart, will give birth to sin.

Being tempted is not a sin, but when we yield ourselves to temptation, then it is considered a sin.

If we are victorious over temptation, then Satan is a defeated foe.

The best response when we are tempted to commit sin is to resist by saying no.

When Satan comes with his temptations and snares, the best weapon that gives us sure victory is to surround ourselves with the Word of God and apply it to our situation.

A lie has no power unless we have subjected ourselves to its deceit.

If our minds are always fixed on Christ, then temptation will cease to lose its power.

If we tend to behold the things of the carnal nature, then temptation would easily beset us, but if we willingly grasp the things that are of the Spirit, then we would easily restrain ourselves from sinful temptations.

Where there is pure love in the heart, the energy of temptation is outwitted by the outpouring of love that is within the heart.

Temptation is the gateway that leads to sin, while sin leads us further into eternal damnation where death presides.

The paradigm of Satan's temptation involves the lust of eyes, the lust of the flesh, and the pride of life.

Being true to God's Word is a lifesaver when it comes to dealing with fierce temptations.

A radical standing for the truth will not compromise our integrity or faith with sinful intrusion.

We can depend upon Jesus to grant us the power to resist the influences that come from Satan's temptations.

If there is no desire for sin in our hearts, then righteousness will prevail over the heights of sinful temptation.

Where there is obedience to God's will and principles, there will always be light.

Being Used by God

God does not need our capabilities to accomplish His will, but rather He desires our availability to be used by Him.

Life is filled with shortcomings, but if we dedicate ourselves to honor God's purpose by giving up our prize possessions to meet the cause of sharing the gospel, surely then our reward will be much greater.

For us to comprehend God's will we must be willing to empty ourselves and let the Holy Spirit fill us with His divine influence, thereby fully grasping the will of God.

God uses the ordinary to bring about His extraordinary purpose to save the lost from dying.

When God calls a person to complete a task, He equips them to fulfill each obligation.

Consider it an eternal privilege to be in service to God, as a servant to a royal King.

It takes all of our strength and faithfulness to remain resolute to God's cause in achieving His goodness and perfect will.

For God to give us sanction, we must allow Him to do the work of intervention on our behalf that His mercies might accomplish what we are unable to do for ourselves.

We have all received the great commission to endorse the gospel by testifying of its truth as a witness to Christ's love and character.

Sometimes our lives are the only light that comes from Christ that people will ever see or experience to tell the tale of Jesus' love.

We must always allow ourselves to be vessels for charity, that our good works might give testimony to Christ's humility and compassion.

It is easier to love with our lips than to love by our actions, but love can only reach its peak if it is expressed both ways.

If there is a sympathizing spirit in our hearts for sin, then the issue of our loyalty to God is in question, because a double-minded person can never stay truly committed to God.

The subject of surrendering ourselves to God includes putting aside our own desires and motives to suit God's own will.

It is necessary to apply the Word of God in decision-making so that good counsel will be able to guide our steps on the right path.

The Nature of Humility

The pattern of God's love revolves around humility, which exploits God's meekness where the essence of His character is seen.

When we humble ourselves, it is easier to be exalted, for God blesses those who have a serene heart, but those who exalt themselves shall be put to shame.

It takes a great amount of humility to face diversities of all kinds and yet still remain calm under difficult circumstances.

If the object of peace is centered in our hearts, then it is difficult for worldly strife and conflict to affect us.

The good thing about courage is that it gives us the strength to admit that we are wrong and the guts to say we are sorry.

Humility is won through the subjection of self to appease God's own goodness, which identifies unselfish motives within our human nature.

In Christ's humility and love, He gave up His own life, irrespective of Himself, to save mankind from the power of sin.

True humility cannot be guided by mere words, but rather actions that stem from charity and goodwill.

If there is no attempt to give support toward the cause of God, then there can be no space for humility in our hearts.

Modesty helps to define a man's character where uniqueness and humbleness are conjoined to bring about good behavior.

Hospitality and kindness welcome God's favor, but cruelty shuts out the presence of God's grace to grant us peace.

There is much strength in forgiveness, for it covers a multitude of sins.

If we are hardened against God's humility, which is offered in grace, it simply means we have allowed sin to take control.

There is hope in humility when Christ is in it, and humility will become a pathway that gives entrance to Christ's heart.

The wisdom of the foolish bears no fruit, but the wisdom of the wise is fruitful unto salvation.

Increase in Wisdom

Wisdom gives foresight for us that is beyond the common knowledge of man, revealing to us the knowledge of God.

The eyes of man are fixed on the things that are gained from this world, while the eyes of those who are fixed on Christ will receive salvation.

If we allow God's wisdom to guide our steps, surely righteousness is conveyed in our hearts.

The worth of wisdom goes beyond the wealth of the world and is weighed in eternity.

The wisdom of God is ignored by the foolish because their minds are depraved and lacking spiritual content.

If we want to inhale wisdom, it is very important for us not to take in things that are contradictory to the teachings of Christ.

Bearing the character of Christ involves total surrender, where our minds are confined to the state of moral reasoning.

Maturity is acquired through submission to God's counsel, which helps us to experience internal growth.

Wisdom does not compromise right for wrong, but it distinguishes between both.

It is good to exercise self-control, for this exerts humility, which bears the fruit of the Spirit.

It is not wise to give way to obsession, for this clouds the mind with corruptible tendencies, which drives forward lust and covetousness.

Love not the things that are associated with sin or else you will be found guilty of spiritual adultery.

If we choose not to make God our first priority then we have created for ourselves an idol before God.

Follow not the ways of the heathen and quote not his words, for in doing so we taint our character.

Seek not to rely on worldly attributes, but cast your cares on the Lord, for His goodness and mercies never fail.

God Honors Right Motives

Secular things are not rooted in the will and testimonies of God; therefore, our motives should be of pure reasoning, which intertwines with God's purpose.

When we rely on ourselves for survival and dependence, selfish motives drive us to conceit, and we choose self above God.

Making right decisions should not be based on emotional or trivial matters, but rather on doing what is morally right in the sight of God.

When people are facing huge challenges and stress, our approach toward them should be one of compassion and humility, which is embedded in the love of Christ.

Choosing to accept God should not be based on what God has to offer us in riches, but rather what we are willing to submit to Him in love.

God does not look on the outcome of how many souls are being won through the gospel, but rather the effort that is being made for them to be saved.

Spiritual gifts are not given for the purpose of gaining wealth, but rather edifying the church and glorifying God.

If God sees that our heart is in the right place to fulfill His will and advance His cause, surely God will commend us for it.

Giving out of charity from the heart is most welcoming to God, for God loves a cheerful giver.

It is not so much about our words making an impact in a person's life, but rather our words materializing in practical actions where they would be fruitful for others to reap the benefits.

If God turns His face away from our motives, it is because we have diverted our interests and desires away from His perfect will.

If our motives are based on the frail suggestions of others whose intakes are not morally correct, then our reasoning becomes unstable.

It is best not to lean on our own understanding but to allow ourselves to be carried away by God's counsel and teachings.

Our stewardship and intellect should be confined to the direction of God's superior wisdom and strength.

The Chain of Prayer

When we pray with sincerity, the courts of heaven listen attentively to our prayers in wonder as God responds to our requests.

Our daily prayers bring us into a holy communion with God and give us added support and strength during the course of the day.

Prayer is essential to the soul, giving nourishment and vigor in the innermost part of the soul.

The affirmation of prayer is the resounding hope that is expressed from our hearts toward God as He awaits our prayers in a gracious manner, demonstrating His unconditional love for us.

A man after God's own heart meditates his mind on praying continuously as he delights himself in the Lord.

Prayer was never intended to revolve around one's self, but rather to make the acquaintance of others who are in need of intercessory prayers.

What makes a prayer powerful is the connection between the one who prays and God.

It takes a fervent prayer that is carried by faith to bring change—the Lord honors such a prayer when it is offered in faith.

Doubt in prayer can sometimes block our prayers because there is a lack of trust in Jesus.

Prayer is a product of the outpouring of our hearts, which consoles the inner thoughts of a man's character.

Where there is much prayer, there is much power, for prayer taps heaven for its power.

If there is no prayer, then there can be no aid or relief in our circumstances, for prayer is our emergency lifeline.

Where there is prayer, faith does not relinquish itself, but enhances its hope in God's unchanging promises.

Miracles are achieved through the eyes of faith, where prayers are offered up with a heart of sincerity and love.

The prayers of the righteous are like astounding truths that do not waver under the attempts of disbelief.

The task of prayer must always be confined to our faith in Christ and not in our own initiatives.

Persecuted but Not Forsaken

God did not promise that we won't encounter difficult circumstances, but He promises to take us through them, for He will neither leave us nor forsake us.

Our trials and tribulations might seem insurmountable, but God's grace and power is sufficient to give us deliverance.

Jesus has not forgotten our struggles or pain, but His peace will help us find rest through the midst of our storm.

We must learn to exercise faith and endurance in Christ as we undergo fiery trials, as Jesus seeks to give us aid.

Sin in the hands of man brings him ruin, while obedience to Christ in the hands of man brings him eternal life.

The outcome of trials can give us stronger results than what we might have anticipated, drawing us closer to God.

Though we are persecuted and afflicted, we are never alone, for Christ surrounds us with the hospitality of His grace and the simplicity of love.

A word from the wise: any challenges we face with uncertainty should be left in the hands of Christ for Him to take charge of the situation.

Where there is war, we must bestow peace, and where there is confusion, we must seek to find order so that there might be stability.

If we are being oppressed or abused by the adversary, it is not in our interest to avenge, but leave all vengeance to God, for He is our mighty avenger.

If our intent is to do good, then surely good will return to us; if it is evil we pursue, then calamity shall reach our houses. For every action, surely there is a reaction.

When faced with crucibles and harsh times, we should take refuge in the Lord, for His comfort will bring us safety and strength where it is needed the most.

Blessed is he who suffers persecution for the sake of Christ's righteousness, for he has gained access to the kingdom of heaven and its rewards.

Much prayer is needed in times of afflictions, as Jesus becomes our mediator, intervening on our behalf.

Redeemed

Accepting Jesus Christ as our Lord and Savior brings us into His marvelous light where we behold His perfect gift of redemption, which He has bestowed on us.

To experience freedom from the power of sin, we must come to accept the truth that is in Christ Jesus, for only by the truth can we be set free.

Although crucifixion by no means is considered an honorable death, it was by this means that Christ shed His blood that we might be fully redeemed.

In no way can we earn salvation through our own righteousness, for it is a free gift that God gave to us through His Son, Jesus Christ, who is our risen Savior.

A redeemed life consists of obedience to Christ's principles and teachings, where His decree has become our constitution.

Before we can ever live a sanctified life, we must reconcile ourselves to God first that we might receive justification through Christ.

If we are redeemed, sin no longer has any power over us, for we have received liberty through Christ's grace, which has made us more than conquerors.

The power of Christ's blood is sufficient to cleanse us of all our iniquities and immoral sins.

An overcomer's life begins and ends with Christ, for whether we live or die we belong to Christ.

Walking with Christ entails a life of submission and devotion toward striving to become like Christ.

As long as we are redeemed by Christ, Satan has no right to bring accusations against God's remnant, for our sins have been erased.

Satan has no power over a man's choice to accept Jesus Christ as his personal Lord and Savior.

Being born-again involves a life of charity and love, where all things are made new, including a transformed character, which is modeled after Christ's character.

Consecrating ourselves to Christ means a total surrender to His supremacy, as well as the neglecting of sin.

A lifetime connection with Christ entails the duty of honoring our commitment through the means of obedience, love, and faith.

A wise man takes heed to acquire moral change that will impact his life unto salvation.

He who lives by Christ's righteousness no longer continues in sin, for God's ways are now his own.

Developing a Christlike Character

Learning to exercise patience teaches us meekness, which highlights the definition of a good character.

Each time we stand out against the injustice or ill-treatment of the less fortunate, Christ's character is being illustrated.

Where love is concerned, there is no line of segregation, but hearts striving to attain peace and unity.

It is best to do right even if the odds are against you—so long as there is a God, He shall reward you.

If our relationship with God is right, then love for our neighbors should be realized, for God is the pioneer of love.

It is not good to gossip or to be judgmental, for this portrays a misguided accuser.

We can possess all the spiritual gifts that God has to offer us, but if we have not love, these gifts are meaningless.

A sincere heart gives way to praying lips; where there is much prayer, there is much aid.

We must never make the problems and affairs of the world a religion, but rather, we must cast all our cares upon Jesus and let Him be our primary focus.

The appreciation for God's love and care should be seen through the act of moral character being displayed in good deeds toward each man.

The Lord beseeches us to live godly lives that we might live to glorify His name.

A love of hatred and evil has no place among God's people, for God despises unlawful behavior that corrupts the nature of man.

There is nothing secretive about sharing God's love, for if we desire to love then love would be plainly seen through our actions.

A forgiving heart reflects God's mercy to blot out our sins—forgiveness is at the heart of God's love.

There is nothing Satan can do or say to corrupt a man's character; a man's actions show his character.

The studying of God's Word prepares our mind to engage in spiritual warfare.

A Callous Heart

When sin is cherished in the heart, it gives way to hardening, and righteous reasoning is difficult to comprehend for the mind has become interlocked with sin.

If our focus is steered toward sin, then our character will seek to adapt its very own nature.

The eye of a man's soul is seen through his heart, which portrays his own character, and if the heart seeks corruption, then the soul has sinned against God.

A mind that is filled with obsession can never obtain the mind of Christ, for obsession gives way to sinful tendencies.

If our aim is to achieve a Christlike character by God's grace, then God will make it possible for our heart of stone to become a heart of flesh.

A heart that is rooted in sin can never come to know God because it desires the carnal nature rather than God.

Satan is so entrenched with sin that he is in bondage to sin; he has mastered sin and now he has become a slave to his own sin.

We can never fully see God's perfect plan if our hearts are held captive by the power of sin.

If we surrender ourselves to the influence of the Holy Spirit, then our hearts will experience true transformation that will result in our salvation.

What man desires in his heart becomes his treasure; therefore, it is best for him to store up that which is good so that he might reap the fruits of righteousness that will be beneficial toward his salvation.

The foolish man says in his heart that there is no God, but the wise man conceives in his heart the existence of God.

A callous heart is tainted with selfish motives giving heed to immoral ambition, but a heart that is bent on self-denial gives way to honoring our commitment to the Lord.

The work of covetousness and envy is conceived from the heart that covers itself with deceitful temptations.

A man who allows his hate to control him finds it difficult to attain peace in his own heart because his mind wanders after iniquity.

It is wise to follow instruction closely as it relates to God's influence and counsel.

Meeting God's Expectation

There is a call to everyone's life as God ordains each man's purpose to consecrate themselves toward God's goodwill that they might in return receive for themselves a crown of life.

God looks inward and knows the deepest thoughts of man; He takes into consideration that man was given morality by nature to distinguish between good and bad behavior, which makes him aware of sin, so he is without excuse.

It is expected of us to keep God's commandments in obedience, for this is the whole duty of man.

Loving God and others are the greatest among the moral laws, for this is what drives humility within the human race.

Charity should be at the heart of each man, otherwise he will not gain favor from God, for God is the giver of charity.

We must lead by God's example and allow His counsel to direct our path, as our lives testify to His glory.

Committing ourselves to God depends on our willingness to honor Him out of love and not selfish ambition.

It is easy to say that we love God, but how many of us show love toward Him with our actions by keeping His commandments.

God expects us to be honest and upright in our affairs; whether in business or personal matters, we must represent God to the fullest in all we do.

For us to unlock God's promises, we must demonstrate the act of faith, for faith is the road that leads to all possibilities.

God wants us to have a zeal for sharing the gospel so that others might come to know God's truth and salvation.

Never compromise God's truth for the sake of others, but hold fast to that which is true and everlasting.

Love neither the world nor the things of the world, for those who find favor with the world, the love of the Father is not in them.

A lying tongue can never appease God whose words are ever trustworthy and truthful.

When we make God's will our own, then our motives will be in the right place.

The Power of God's Word

If we should apply ourselves to the influence of God's Word, then our lives would be saturated by its transforming power, which will surely convert our souls to Christ.

The words of God make wise the foolish because they gain increasing knowledge that will illuminate the pathway to salvation.

There is life in God's words for they are Spirit, and in them flows a fountain of youth that sustains life.

If we should seek the counsel of God's Word when issues arise in our lives, they would easily subside.

God's wisdom adds to each man's intellect, enabling him to become wiser, where his status might attain spiritual maturity.

The words of God serve many purposes, including instruction, teaching, reproof, and reconciliation.

The Word of God is a path unto our feet and a direction unto our journey, which helps to complete each man's destiny.

Those who refuse to honor God's Word by keeping His commandments fall in the category of hopelessness, where heaven's door is closed to those who choose not to accept His words.

The power of God's Word is demonstrated through His love as rendered by the power of Christ's crucifixion and resurrection.

Every promise that is written through God's Word is kept according to His perfect will so that they might be fulfilled under His grace as a gift to us, revealing His character.

If we are driven by the Word of God, then surely we are under the influence of the Holy Spirit, for He is the one who inspires us all.

Knowing God involves keeping His commandments, for no man can love God and not keep His commandments.

If we meditate upon the Word of God, surely we would be able to renew our minds and replenish our hearts with the countenance of His words.

When we exhibit God's Word, we are revealing to the world the nature of God's awesome love and character.

The Word of God is beyond the reasoning or philosophy of man, for the virtues of God's wisdom and power is much greater than any man.

Self Ambition

It was the power of sin that drove Satan into rebellion against God as he was motivated by his own selfish desires that led to his fall from grace.

We can never be led by our own explanations or intellect to sustain ourselves; we require the intervention of God's grace and mercy.

There is no way doubts can ever cure our fears, but by faith in Christ, we are made more than conquerors through Him.

When our intentions are carried by self-purpose to the exclusion of God's will, for our own glory, it is considered treason against God.

It is not God's intention for any of us to determine His will for another person's life, otherwise we are guilty of committing sin.

Our aim should be accomplishing God's will so that our lives might have true meaning, enjoying the vastness of God's glory and splendor.

For us to experience humility in Christ, we must be able to have a willing heart to share with those who are in need.

We are not obligated to give aid to a snared conscience, but rather give welcome to moral reasoning where the mind of Christ is sound.

Love can never be fully felt if there is only selfish ambition stored up in our hearts.

Those who are in pursuit of greed allow themselves to be caught by worldly attire and fame, which drives them to acquire more.

It is not possible for a person to please God while his heart craves after the lust of the flesh and sexual immorality.

Satan gets angry with the idea that his attempt to mislead us fails as we subject ourselves to God's protective influence.

There is no doubt that when we put our trust in God, self-denial becomes our primary motive in honoring our commitment to God.

There is no need for us to rely in the hope of others, but to be assured that we can always count on Jesus to give aid to our situation.

Greed is a detrimental hazard to our moral salvation.

We cannot be walking with God and holding the devil's hand at the same time—we are either with God or against Him.

Preparation for God's Kingdom

Life here on earth will soon come to an end when Jesus returns to receive His children in glory.

The kingdom of God belongs to those who possess it through the gift of salvation, which is purchased for us through Jesus Christ.

We must be born of the water through baptism by immersion and be born of the Spirit through the indwelling of the Holy Spirit before we can enter the kingdom of heaven.

Conversion of the heart begins with earnest repentance before forgiveness can be conveyed for one to obtain pardon from sin.

For our journey to heaven to be successful, we must totally surrender to Christ and renounce our sins.

The life we live now will determine whether or not we will gain entry into God's kingdom; therefore, our lives must be consecrated to Christ's own character.

If our eyes are fixed on temporal things, then our will to experience faith in regards to heavenly things will diminish.

It is good to have wealth when God is placed above the means of our riches, but if not, our wealth will become a curse to us, just as a snare would entangle our minds.

One of man's greatest weaknesses is his own sin, but if he can master his own sin, then in his weakness he will become strong.

We know not the hour of Jesus' coming and there is no repentance in the grave; therefore, it is best to give our lives to Christ before it is too late.

The wise man knows that there is power in accepting Jesus Christ as his Savior, but the foolish man sees no need for a Savior and accepts his folly as good fortune.

The only thing that can prevent us from entering God's kingdom is our poor choice to serve Satan.

The kingdom of God begins with accepting Jesus in our hearts, and it ends with Christ's eternal glory.

Before we can experience true reformation, we must engage in a spiritual revival that awakens our desire to know Christ.

Protocol

We must never seek to endorse any argument when there is a dispute or disagreement among persons, for this will add tension to what already exists.

It must never be our intention to seek out the faults of others while using it against them in the spirit of opposition for our own selfish purposes.

If we remain faithful to Christ and imitate His character, then by no means can the devil enter in.

Our conduct should be guided by an atmosphere of love and humility where our character can impact the lives of others in a positive way so that God might receive glory.

If hatred finds comfort in our hearts, then the carnal nature has dominion over us because we have welcomed its presence.

It is not right for us to blame God for what sin has imparted or contributed to the painful consequences we are facing.

When things go wrong, our first reaction should be to consult God for aid or a solution to the problem.

We should always welcome everything that God does because God knows what is best for each individual.

In regards to sinful temptations and snares, we should show no emotions or remorse, for this fuels Satan's plot and conspiracy.

We must never plan a person's downfall or ruin, but we must leave all vengeance unto God.

If injustice is done to us, then we should allow God to be the one who will seek justice on our behalf.

It is everyone's responsibility to keep God's covenant as we remain obedient to His commandments.

It is better to be a pauper than to have riches with no salvation, for what is precious to man and still affords him no salvation.

The main function of God's conduct is to exert love; if love is at the heart of each man, then God's work of goodwill is accomplished.

A man who knows God knows that God does not compromise His truth but desires for everyone to live according to His truth.

A Message for God's People

Do not be stubborn or refuse to be a witness of My truth to other people.

Conform yourselves not to the ways of this world nor its traditions, for God considers not their corruptible ways.

Have nothing to do with partaking in evil matters, otherwise you will find yourselves guilty, awaiting God's judgment.

God will not withhold discipline from those He loves once they have gone astray and contrary to His will.

When it comes to truth, the majority is excused, for the truth is more than anyone can handle, for God is truth.

It is not good to put our hands to the Lord's work and then turn away from carrying out its mandate as God requires.

God will hold us accountable for refusing prophecy, for this quenches the Spirit; we must always endorse God's truth with charity.

We must never allow our own expectations to define God's will or purpose but rather accept everything as God instructed.

If we claim to love God yet love not our neighbors, then the love that we have claimed is in vain, for love has no barriers.

Do not make any idol for yourself, for this betrays your love for the God who has always been faithful to you.

Evil can never defeat the armor of love, for it cannot be penetrated when it comes to love, for love is infinite.

Be watchful for your enemy, the devil; he seeks to plunge you into sin that he might claim you as his own.

Be not fearful of things to come, but trust in God, for He holds the future as His own.

If God is for us, who can be against us? God is our shield; we have found refuge and defense against our enemies.

We must never assume that it was our own efforts or power that gave us victory over sin, but only through the blood of Christ was it made possible for us to have triumph over sin.

Sin Ruins

Where there is sin, death is not far behind, for the wages of sin is death. If we have chosen to surrender ourselves to Christ's own righteousness, then there is only life to gain.

Because of sin the world is experiencing uncertainties; where sin diminishes because of hope, the world loses its power.

Let no one tell you that your sins are too big, but count on Jesus who is our sin bearer and friend.

If we remain in Christ, sin will not so easily beset us—its purpose to ruin us is defeated through Christ's intervention.

Sin can never produce anything good, for its fruits are filled with all manner of evil that destroys the integrity of the soul.

The only guard we have against sin is to refrain from it through the power of Christ, who grants us the victory over sin.

Never allow your sins to hold you captive; you are worth more to God than the cost of sin, which is death.

If it was left to sin, this world would have been done away with, but because of Christ's intervention and His sacrificial blood, this world received the birth of a new hope, that through Him restoration to the eternal chain is made possible again.

Sin separates us from God; nothing with its impurity can stand before the presence of the Lord's glory and remain untouched, for God is like a consuming fire.

Satan's waywardness drives each man to sin, but if we are grounded in Christ, along with His power, then we will be able to resist the tempter's snare.

If we allow sin to control our lives, then we have welcome death to enter our souls, which will leave us without a trace of salvation.

The terror that sin causes is refined to Satan's work of evil; for us to find refuge in the midst of trouble, we must confine ourselves to Christ.

Sin is no respecter of persons, and if we want to have sure victory over the power of sin, we must put on the character of Christ so that we might resist the elements of sin.

God loves the person who has committed sin, but He hates sin because it is the only thing that separates us from God.

If It Was Not for God's Grace

While the law of God demands justice, grace demands the hand of God's mercy, for grace exceeds the law.

Grace is the result of God's unmerited love, which is unconditionally expressed through the favor of His humility and compassion.

Grace is the substance of hope that is rooted in Christ's love, which is given to us as a free gift of God's declarative mercy.

God's grace comes with boundaries; His grace will not always strive with man because the abusing of its power causes God's judgment to be exerted.

If it was not for God's grace, humanity would have perished long ago under the power of the law's death penalty.

When God answers our prayers, it is a congruity of His grace, which responds to our sincere act of faith.

God's open arm of love helps us to experience grace even when we are undeserving of it; God still bestows His grace upon us.

If God's grace reaches us and we choose to turn our hearts away from the pleading of His Spirit, despite the out pouring of His love, it will eventually become an unpardonable sin.

Grace does not depend on us but on God's intentions for our own good that we might benefit from its power.

Where there is true repentance in the heart, God's grace is not far; if it is not genuine, then the wrath of God will show its face.

If God gives us grace then we should receive it in charity, for this shows reverence to God's love and authority.

If God does not find it difficult to offer us grace, then why should we find it so hard to show someone else grace.

God prefers mercy than sacrifices for mercy covers a multitude of sins.

Know that the Lord is good and His mercy endures, but never mistake God's grace for our own foolish mistakes.

Thank God all the more for His sustaining grace, which has kept us alive and well.

Who Receives the Glory?

We can never take full credit for our success because God is the one who gives us the capability and talent to achieve success.

It is never in man's own strength to resist the power of temptation, but it is the result of Christ's own strength that gives us the victory.

It is better to humble ourselves than to be boastful, for exalting ourselves can lead us to a fall, but meekness lifts a man up.

The thing that conquers a man is his own choice, so if we choose to accept Jesus as Lord, then to God be the glory. If the choice is Satan, may God help us because the result will be devastating.

No man can honor God by rejecting His words, for this proves him unworthy before God and man.

Having good titles behind our names will not grant us favor in heaven, but by representing God's character we might receive favor from the host of heaven.

We can never justify ourselves by self-exaltation as Lucifer did, for this covets the supremacy of God's authority and majesty.

All the riches in the world, whether wealth or possessions, belong to God because He created all things.

A man's own selfishness exalts himself, but if he opens his heart to charity, then God is exalted, for it is better to give than to receive.

When calamity strikes, do we still honor God or do we blame Him for it? Whether in the good or bad times, God should be praised.

Only those who understand what it means to love can really appreciate love when it is shown, for this exalts God.

It is not good to impersonate those who acknowledge themselves rather than God, for this is self-seeking.

God's reputation does not depend on man, but man's reputation and livelihood depends on God; man is neither independent of God nor is he capable of leading himself.

Never should you doubt God's faithfulness for fables or self-indulgence, but allow God to receive His due glory.

Does Jesus Care

While we were yet sinners Jesus made His grace available to us through the plan of redemption; His atonement exceeds the power of sin, which gave us freedom from sin.

Because Jesus lives we can face our problems head-on, knowing that His love and care will help carry us through.

The ordeals and trials we undergo are temporary, yet the peace that Jesus gives is more filling than our challenges.

Why should we fear or be discouraged when we know we have a Savior who is always near.

Jesus does not hate others because of their hatred toward Him, but yet His hatred is against sin.

We are never alone; the warmth of God's love surrounds us, and His compassion keeps us secure in His care.

We can count on Jesus to be our shield and refuge; in Him we can find deliverance from the terror of sudden tragedy.

When faced with uncertainties, we should put our trust in Jesus, knowing He will attend to our cares, making His will available to us.

While temporary things are replaceable, God's care over us is irreplaceable because it never ceases.

What God has given to us as a gift through His Son, Jesus Christ, is truly a miracle of grace that ignites salvation.

Jesus listens attentively to the earnest prayers of those who are in need; He sympathizes with their pain and wants.

Where there is sadness, Jesus' joy is not far, and where there is righteousness, eternity is at its heart.

If we would open our hearts enough to Jesus' love, then it would be enough for us to accept Him as Lord and Savior.

Jesus does not need to prove His love to us; the fact that we are living speaks volume of His love for us.

The constraint of sin is not for us to bear alone; Jesus is ever interceding on our behalf.

Lessons Taken From the Holy Spirit

We can never be too sure of life's expectation, whether it involves calamity or good fortune, but our hope should be confined to God's will, knowing that whatever comes our way we are confident of God's love and care over us.

When we consecrate ourselves to the Holy Spirit, we are likely to acquire two things: life transformation and victory over our sinful nature.

The influence of the Holy Spirit does not subject itself to falsehood or deceit, for this influence is established in perfect truth.

We must always ensure that we commit ourselves to whatever the Spirit wants us to do, for this proves our usefulness and loyalty to Him.

We cannot possess the Spirit of God and still devote ourselves to the carnal nature, for this is treachery to God.

If we cannot learn to forgive others of their sins, how then should we expect God to forgive us of our sins?

Forgive and you shall be forgiven, for forgiveness covers a multitude of sins. As you forgive, God in return will forgive you too.

It is our duty to rid ourselves of whatever grieves the Holy Spirit or else we have no peace with God.

If we confine ourselves to the things of this world and its sinful practices, then the Holy Spirit will seek to leave us. For what does godliness have to do with ungodliness or what does light have to do with darkness?

A person who is driven by the Holy Spirit must never seek to compromise his or her own faith for the enjoyment of sinful pleasure.

It makes no sense to fight against what God wills, for whatever God speaks comes to pass. Therefore, it's best to stay out of God's way.

If we are convicted of sin by the Holy Spirit, we should seek to repent or else we will remain in condemnation.

God will never accuse you of a sin that has already been forgiven, for when God forgives, He does not hold sin against you anymore.

The task of prayer must always be combined with our faith in Christ and not in our own initiatives.

Emphasizing Faith

Every time God makes a willful sacrifice it is His intention to achieve greater good so that His love might be revealed and His name glorified.

The essence of Satan's character is rooted in lies—lying is his native language.

The sooner we accept Jesus Christ as our Lord and Savior the sooner our destiny will be to inherit the kingdom of God.

It takes only the power of God to turn a sinner to repentance.

If we want to know the mind of God, we must consult His Word, and by applying His Word, we become more like Him.

Spiritual warfare is a result of opposition to God's truth, but it is won by allegiance to God's profound truth.

When our minds are troubled with guilt, it leads to shame, but if our hearts will seek remission, then God's forgiveness will comfort the soul.

The true value of compassion is within the nature of God's love and character, which is fortified by His wholesomeness.

If we should seek to lavish ourselves in the countenance of God's wisdom, most certainly we would find refuge.

The imagery of God's love is seen in the ultimate sacrifice of His Son, Jesus Christ.

As God's children we must never compromise the truth for our own convenience or for anyone else's.

Count it as pure joy in honoring God's commands, for this portrays the whole duty of man.

What is popular among the majority is not always considered right, but what is morally correct in the sight of God surmounts all.

If we pursue what is right in the sight of God, then our steps will not be guided by the persuasion of sin.

The aspect of prayers and daily devotion in studying the word of God affirms our faith and commitment toward a loving and caring God.

If we are open to exercise humility among ourselves, then we would be able see God's own love and character at work within us.

Love Surpasses Sin

Love, which is pleasing in the sight of God, despises those things that belong to evil.

Put on the armor of God that you might withstand the evil schemes of Satan.

The love of money corrupts good character, but love for God endorses good favor for eternity.

If love consoles our heart, then it would not be difficult to experience peace in our hearts, because where there is love, peace is never far behind.

Beware of Satan's darts that can even deceive the very elect; we must cling to that which is truth, for only in the truth can we find refuge from Satan's darts.

The power of the Holy Spirit is beyond the control of anyone's authority or power and is beyond all measures.

We invite you to view the complete
selection of titles we publish at:

www.AspectBooks.com

Scan with your mobile
device to go directly
to our website.

Please write or email us your praises, reactions, or
thoughts about this or any other book we publish at:

P.O. Box 954
Ringgold, GA 30736

info@AspectBooks.com

Aspect Books titles may be purchased in bulk for
educational, business, fund-raising, or sales promotional use.
For information, please e-mail:

BulkSales@AspectBooks.com

Finally, if you are interested in seeing
your own book in print, please contact us at:

publishing@AspectBooks.com

We would be happy to review your manuscript for free.

www.ingramcontent.com/pod-product-compliance
Lightning Source LLC
Chambersburg PA
CBHW071227160426
43196CB00012B/2437